World Religions and Beliefs

THE
Birth
OF Islam

A modern mosque built by the Red Sea, in Jeddah, Saudi Arabia

World Religions and Beliefs

THE
Birth
OF Islam

Don Nardo

**MORGAN
REYNOLDS**
PUBLISHING

Greensboro, North Carolina

WORLD
Religions
AND Beliefs

Founders of Faiths

Mystics and Psychics

The Birth of Christianity

The Birth of Islam

World Religions and Beliefs: The Birth of Islam

Library of Congress Cataloging-in-Publication Data

Nardo, Don, 1947-
The birth of Islam / by Don Nardo.
    p. cm. -- (World religions and beliefs)
Includes bibliographical references.
ISBN 978-1-59935-146-9
1. Islam--History--Juvenile literature. 2. Islamic
Empire--History--Juvenile literature. I. Title.
BP55.N27 2011
297.09'021--dc22

                                        2010038442

Printed in the United States of America
First Edition

The Great Mosque of Kairouan, also known as the Mosque of Uqba, is located in Kairouan, Tunisia. The mosque has the oldest-standing minaret—tall spire with conical crown—in the world.

Rows of slender columns and striped arches in the prayer hall of the Great Mosque of Córdoba, in Spain. The former mosque, now a cathedral, is a World Heritage site.

Contents

The name "Allah" written in Arabic calligraphy (from right to left) by seventeenth-century Ottoman artist Hâfiz Osman

Chapter

1

The
Middle East
Before Islam

Islam is the youngest of the world's major faiths, having emerged in the seventh century in the Arabian Peninsula. Although it was the last of the principal religions to form, Islam has grown to include an estimated 1.5 billion followers, known as Muslims, making it the second-largest religion behind Christianity.

Despite its continuous expansion over the centuries—particularly in Europe and the United States, where Muslims make up the fastest-growing religious minority—many people of other faiths know very little about Islam. For example, few know that

in Arabic the word *Islam* means "submission," specifically to God's will. And *Muslim* is the Arabic word for someone who submits to God by becoming a member of the Islamic faith.

British, American, and other Western historians and writers used to call Islam "Muhammadism," a reference to Muhammad, Islam's founder and chief prophet. The term Muhammadism is no longer used, however, because it is inaccurate; it gives the misleading impression that Muslims worship Muhammad as a divine entity, similar to the way that Christians worship Jesus Christ.

On the contrary, Muhammad was (and still is) seen as a human prophet, not the focus of worship. Following his teachings, Muslims practice monotheism, or *din*, and worship one God, whom they call Allah. Like Christians and Jews, scholar Tamara Sonn explains, Muslims "worship one God, believed to be the creator and merciful judge of all humanity. Muslims revere Abraham, Moses, and Jesus, along with other figures familiar to readers of Jewish and Christian scripture [holy writings]." Joined together in this greater tradition of monotheism, Muslims, Jews, and Christians are all spiritual cousins, or what Islam recognizes as *ahl al-kitab*—the "people of the book."

This figurative "book" refers to the scriptures sacred to these faiths—the Old Testament for the Jews; the Old and New Testaments for the Christians; and the Qur'an (or Koran) for the Muslims.

Because Islam is the youngest of these three faiths, the other two strongly influenced its formation. It arose in seventh-century Arabia, which was situated more or less centrally in the Middle East. Arab society and culture was one of the region's three main civilizations, a status it shared with the Byzantines and the Sassanians. All of these cultures, and eventually the rest of the world, would undergo drastic change as a result of Islam's rise to prominence.

The Byzantines

The first of these early medieval Middle Eastern peoples, the Byzantines, did not refer to themselves by that name, which historians assigned to them many centuries later. They called themselves *Rhomaioi,* a Greek word meaning "Romans," and they named their imperial state Basileia Romaion, or "Kingdom of the Romans." This was no idle boast, for the Byzantine Empire, centered in northern Greece and stretching into parts of the Middle East, was the surviving remnant of the old Roman Empire. The latter had once covered much of Europe, North Africa, and the Middle East; but steady decline and finally massive invasions of tribal peoples from northern Europe had taken an awful toll, and the western sector of the Empire collapsed in the late 400s CE.

The eastern part of the realm survived, with its capital at Constantinople, located along the southern shore of the Black Sea. (The term *Byzantine* comes from Byzantium, the older Greek name for Constantinople.) Seeing the western Roman lands in shambles, the eastern emperors sought to regain control of and restore their former territories. For a while, they were fairly successful in this aim. The emperor Justinian, who reigned from 527–565, retook Italy from the tribal Visigoths and brought northwestern Africa and coastal Spain under Byzantine authority. Over time, however, most of the reclaimed western Roman lands again fell to various invading peoples.

Even with these losses, the Byzantine empire long remained strong in the east. Century after century the empire withstood frequent attacks waged by neighboring states and grew to become a huge and influential center of a sophisticated culture. Byzantine paintings, mosaics, architectural achievements, and literary works were reputed as being among the finest in the world; and Byzantine traders carried goods of all kinds to both near and distant lands, maintaining the empire's strong economy.

Furthermore, the Byzantine Empire remained the largest and most splendid surviving enclave of the Christian religion. In hundreds of cathedrals and churches, priests and bishops of the Eastern Orthodox Christian Church continued to promote the worship of Jesus Christ. The church also received strong patronage from Byzantine leaders, who were passionate and emphatic about maintaining and spreading the faith. A law passed by Justinian, for example, required priests to conduct mass and other ceremonies in upraised voices: "We order all bishops and priests to repeat the divine service and the prayer . . . not in an undertone, but in a loud voice which can be heard by the faithful people, in such a way that the [faithful] may be induced to [a] higher appreciation of the praises and blessings of God."

The Sassanians

Very different in many ways was the religion of one of the Byzantines' chief rivals in the Middle East—the Sassanian (or Sassanid) Empire, in Persia. The region known for ages by the general term Persia was centered in Iran and sometimes included parts of neighboring areas, such as Iraq and Afghanistan. The first great Persian Empire, founded by King Cyrus II, lasted from the mid-500s to the 330s BCE. The Macedonian Greek ruler Alexander III (later called "the Great") conquered Persia and much of the rest of the region in the 330s, and Greeks ruled the region until the late 200s and early 100s BCE, when the Parthian kings of Iran rose to power. The Parthians became fierce competitors and enemies of the Roman Empire.

A series of Roman military forays into the Middle East finally pushed the Parthian realm into fatal decline between the early 100s and early 200s CE. Near the end of this dynasty, the Parthian state also experienced setbacks from within, and in 224 one of the Parthian provincial governors seized control of the capital, Ctesiphon (just south of modern Baghdad, Iraq). Assuming the throne name of Ardashir I, he founded the Sassanian Empire.

This new Persian nation, like the Parthian one before it, frequently warred against the Romans in a rivalry that continued

A hand-colored woodcut of a Gustav Dore illustration depicting Alexander the Great discovering the body of Darius III, king of Persia. After Alexander took over Persia, he pursued King Darius, only to find that he had already been killed by a Persian satrap, or governor, named Bessus.

for centuries, even after the fall of Rome's western realm. After Rome fell, this enmity entered a new phase in which the Sassanians and Byzantines competed for control of large portions of the Middle East. In 612, for instance, the Sassanian ruler Khusrau II captured Jerusalem and parts of Palestine, then controlled by the Byzantines. He also attacked the Byzantine capital, Constantinople. In retaliation, a Byzantine army moved rapidly through northern Sassanian territory in 627 and assaulted Ctesiphon. Khusrau died while trying to escape.

During these wars, whichever king was winning at any given moment usually touted the supremacy of his nation and people. In particular, each side believed its religion was superior and "truer" than its enemy's. The Byzantines insisted that they would ultimately prevail because Christ was on their side.

In contrast, the Sassanians, like the original Persians under Cyrus II, practiced a faith known as Zoroastrianism. It was based on the teachings of a prophet named Zarathustra, whom the Greeks later called Zoroaster. Essentially it was monotheistic in that it accepted the existence of a single all-powerful god, Ahura-Mazda, the "wise lord." The faithful held that Ahura-Mazda stood for truth, goodness, and light. Supposedly he was occupied in an endless struggle with a dark and evil force or being (equivalent to the Christian devil) named Ahriman, who stood for disorder and "the lie." By rejecting the lie and accepting God, members of the faith could expect to achieve peace and a successful life, as alluded to in part of a surviving Zoroastrian prayer:

> Do ye, Ahura, grant [us] strength, righteousness, and that Kingdom, Good Thought, whereby [we] may establish pleasant dwellings and peace. I [believe], Mazda, that thou canst bring this to pass. . . . Welcome me for instruction, Mazda, for the great community [of your followers].

ZOROASTRIAN INFLUENCE ON OTHER FAITHS

Some scholars of ancient religions think that certain Zoroastrian ideas, which circulated through the Middle East for many centuries, had an influence on early Christian theology. In this view, God's opposition to Satan (the devil) mirrors the Zoroastrian struggle between the god Ahura-Mazdah and an evil, dark being, Ahriman. In addition to the eternal fight between good and evil, a number of symbolic opposing concepts from Zoroastrian theology are said to have emerged in Christian thinking: comparisons and struggles between light and darkness; battles between angels and demons; and the belief that good people will end up in paradise, while bad people will go to hell. These scholars also point out that several similar ideas appear in Islamic theology, which, because of Arabia's close proximity to Persia, may also have felt the influence of Zoroastrianism.

The Arabs

The third important civilization in the early medieval Middle East was that of the Arabs. They dwelled mainly in the large peninsula named for them, which they referred to as *Jazirat al-Arab*, or "Island of the Arabs."

Large sections of Arabia are extremely arid and feature some of the most forbidding deserts in the world, an environment that had a profound influence on the peninsula's inhabitants. The original Arabs were apparently all nomads who survived the harsh desert environment by taking part in a seasonal migration cycle. During the hot summer months, they stayed put and tried to expend as little energy as possible. Then, starting with the October rains, they spent seven or eight months traveling from one grazing ground to another on the edges of the deserts. For these yearly journeys, they domesticated the camel, an animal able to carry on for long periods of time on very little water.

During the fifth and sixth centuries, however, some Arabs began changing their lifestyles. Those who continued the old nomadic ways came to be known as Bedouins. (That is the English term; the name they use to describe themselves is Bedu.) Those who gave up the nomadic life began settling in permanent towns.

Among the more important of these early towns was Mecca, which would later bear the distinction of being the hometown of Islam's founder, Muhammad. Mecca became an ethnic and religious melting pot, as Christians, Jews, Zoroastrian Persians, and other refugees from neighboring lands settled there. It also emerged as a center of international trade. Local merchants traveled to Byzantine, Sassanian, and Egyptian cities to exchange goods.

In addition, Mecca became early medieval Arabia's center of religious worship and festivities. At this point, the Arabs were polytheistic—each Arab town or tribe had its own god or gods. Over time, they all recognized certain deities and worshiped them in their local towns. But once a year people from all around the peninsula traveled to Mecca, a journey called *hajj*, meaning "pilgrimage," to worship together. The central meeting place was the Kaaba, a large, cube-shaped structure. (It originally may have been built around the remains of a fallen meteorite.) Diverse statues of Arab gods rested inside the Kaaba, and members of the various tribes laid down their arms (if they were then at war) to worship these idols. They also worshiped an overall, supreme divinity they at first referred to as *al-ilah*, meaning simply "the God."

PRE-ISLAMIC MECCA

It is not surprising that Mecca eventually became the center and holiest city of Islam because earlier it had been the principal religious hub of the pre-Islamic Arabs. Their beliefs combined local Arabian concepts and others borrowed from the Jewish and Christian communities that grew up in Mecca. Richard Hooker, formerly of Washington State University, writes that by 500 CE,

> *Mecca had already become a religious center of Arabic culture as its name suggests—one possible derivation of the name, "Mecca," is the word, "makorba," or "temple." The religion of the pre-Islamic Arabs was a mixture of Bedouin polytheism, Judaism, and a little bit of Christianity. The pre-Islamic Arabs worshipped three goddesses, al-Lat, al-Uzza, and Manat, who were all daughters of one god, Allah. This one god was probably derived from the monotheistic religions of Judaism and Christianity.*

The Arabs came to see this deity, whose name evolved into "Allah," as virtually the same supreme god worshiped by the Christians and Jews. There was one difference, however, and this point became a significant source of enmity between followers of the three religions: the Jews had the prophets Abraham and Moses and the Christians had Jesus Christ, but the Arabs had no prophet of their own. Religious scholar Karen Armstrong writes:

> The Jews and Christians whom [the Arabs] met often taunted [them] for being left out of the divine plan. . . . [It] seemed to many of the more thoughtful people in Arabia that the Arabs were a lost people, exiled forever from the civilized world and ignored by God himself.

But whether or not this common perception was true, it was about to change quite drastically. The three leading Middle Eastern civilizations—Byzantine, Persian, and Arab—were about to meet head-on and eventually unite in a way no one could have predicted. That fateful collision would be brought about by a man the Arabs came to see as their own prophet, whom Allah, in his wisdom, had chosen at last as his messenger to the "lost people" of Arabia: Muhammad of Mecca.

The painting *Ansicht von Mekka in Arabien* by Hubert Sattler depicts a view of Mecca and the Kaaba circa 1897. The painting is on display at the Salzburg Museum in Salzburg, Austria.

21

The name "Muhammad" in traditional Thuluth calligraphy (a form of Islamic calligraphy) by Hattat Aziz Efendi, an Ottoman calligrapher

Chapter

2

Emergence
of the Final
Prophet

During the month of Ramadan in 610 CE, a forty-year-old merchant lay asleep in a cave near the town of Mecca, not far from the shore of the Red Sea in southwestern Arabia. Suddenly, a loud voice awakened him. The source of that voice, what it said, and how the merchant reacted soon changed his life and altered the framework and future of his entire society. Journalist and Middle East scholar Lesley Hazleton points out that Arabia was already "poised to step out of the background as a political and cultural backwater and take a major role on the world stage." Judaism and Christianity had been on that stage for centuries.

Now, through the revelation and leadership of a Meccan merchant, their monotheistic faith—Islam—was born; and it would endure a tumultuous beginning and flourish as a major world religion.

Childhood and Family

The merchant in the cave was Muhammad, whose name means "worthy of praise." (His name is also spelled "Muhammed" or "Mohammed," but "Muhammad" is transliterated from the Arabic and is the variant most commonly used in English.) He was a member of the Hashim clan of the larger Quraysh tribe of Arabs. He had spent his entire life in Mecca, where most of the prominent citizens belonged to the Quraysh. Like so many others in Mecca, they were predominantly merchants and traders who made their livings from the prosperous trade route that ran north-to-south through western Arabia.

Trade was not the only way the Quraysh made their money. They also took advantage of Mecca's status as a central gathering point of worshipers from across the Arabian peninsula. They "skillfully melded faith and finance," Hazleton explains, "charging fees for access to the Kaaba, tolls on trade caravans, and taxes on commercial transactions. But the wealth they generated was not shared by all." The idea of sharing wealth, a basic principle of tribal organization, did not continue in the new urban context; and this change proved to be pivotal. "While some clans within the tribe prospered, others did not. It was these others with whom Muhammad's message would first resonate."

Muhammad was born in Mecca in about 570. His father had passed away before he was born and his mother died when he was six, leaving his paternal grandfather, Abdul Muttalib, to raise him. After his grandfather died in 578, Muhammad's uncle, Abu Talib, took charge of the boy. Not much is known about Muhammad's childhood, and most scholars agree that he likely grew up a poor, unassuming shepherd. Eventually, it appears, he joined some of his tribal brethren in the merchant business.

At about the age of twenty-five, Muhammad married a well-to-do widow named Khadija, who was fifteen years older. They had six children together. Four of them, daughters Zaynab, Ruqayya, Fatima, and Umm Kulthum, made it into adulthood. Although polygamy was legal in Arabia at that time, Khadija, whom Muhammad was said to have adored, remained his only wife until she died in 619.

The Voice and the Qur'an

Little for certain is known about Muhammad's young adult years, though it is certain that he belonged to a group of Meccan men known as *hanif.* They were dissatisfied with the prevailing religious beliefs and customs. And from time to time each of them retreated alone to the countryside to meditate.

It was during one of these retreats that Muhammad entered a cave on Mount Hira, not far from Mecca, and fell asleep. After a while, he felt himself jolted into a waking state.

Cave Hira in Mecca

A booming voice told him he was God's messenger, but the startled Muhammad had no idea what that meant and reacted fearfully. "I was standing," he later recalled, "but I fell on my knees and crawled away, my shoulders trembling." He ran out of the cave, hurried home to his wife, Khadija, and told her, "Cover me! Cover me!" perhaps hoping to hide from the terrifying voice.

At first, Muhammad was worried that an evil spirit might have visited him—so worried that he momentarily thought about taking his own life. However, the being behind the mysterious voice, an impressive human-like figure, suddenly appeared and identified himself as the angel Gabriel. The angel once more informed Muhammad that he was God's messenger and then ordered him to begin reciting. Confused, Muhammad asked, "What shall I recite?" But the angel abruptly seized him and words began to pour from Muhammad's mouth. "Recite: in the name of thy Lord Who created," he blurted out, "created Man of a blood-clot. Recite: And thy Lord is the Most Generous who taught by the Pen, taught Man that he knew not."

Al Fatiha, the first sura, or chapter, of the Qur'an, the holy book of Islam

The angel told Muhammad that the words he had recited had come directly from God. Moreover, because Muhammad was God's messenger, or prophet, it was his duty to pass God's words on to other people. Over time, the angel made numerous other visits. In each visit Muhammad received a few more divinely inspired words and phrases, and together these sayings comprised the holy Qur'an (or Koran), which means "recitation." In all, there were 114 *suras,* or chapters, containing 6,236 *ayat,* or verses.

THE NIGHT OF POWER

Muslims across the world annually celebrate the holy month of Ramadan, which begins on a different date each year. The twenty-seventh day of Ramadan is called the Night of Power (Laylat al-Qadr). It commemorates the night in 610 when Muhammad received his first revelation from the angel Gabriel (called Jibreel in the Qur'an). The ninety-seventh sura in the Qur'an, often referred to as "The Grandeur," says the following about that fateful night:

We [God] have indeed revealed this [Message] in the Night of Power: And what will explain to thee what the Night of Power is! The Night of Power is better than a thousand months. Therein come down the angels and the Spirit [Gibreel] by Allah's permission, on every errand: Peace!... This until the rise of the morn.

As a result of these experiences, Muhammad came to believe that he actually was a prophet of Allah. In fact, he claimed to be the final prophet of several that God had inspired over the course of many centuries. Previous prophets had included, among others, Adam, Noah, Abraham, Moses, and Jesus. None of the prophets, including Muhammad, were themselves divine; instead, they had been chosen by God as instruments of revelation to deliver his words to humanity.

Many followers of these earlier messengers, Muhammad said, had gone astray and become confused about their beliefs. The purpose of the Qur'an was to put God's followers back on the right religious path, so to speak. Because he did not know how to read or write, Muhammad did not write down the verses of the Qur'an that came to him over the years. Rather, he repeated them to others, and some of those others memorized them. The initial transmission of Islam's sacred book, therefore, was oral.

The central messages of the Qur'an, Muhammad learned, were simple but extremely powerful. First, there is only one God—not multiple gods, as the Arabs had long believed. Second, all men and women should submit completely to God's will, a

The cover of a Qur'an

concept made clear by the name of the faith—Islam, meaning submission to God. Third, although Allah judges people strictly, he also forgives them for their sins. So showing complete obedience to God can, under certain circumstances, erase the effects of sin.

Early Converts and Persecution

Even before he had received all of the words of the Qur'an, Muhammad was already enthusiastic about the messages he believed were coming from God. And he wasted no time in sharing these messages with others. He told Khadija, who became the first convert to the new religion. The next converts were Muhammad's ten-year-old cousin, Ali ibn Abi Talib; his adopted son, Zaid ibn Haritha; and his close friend, Abu Bakr. The number of Meccans who privately converted and became Muslims remained relatively small for three years. It was then that Muhammad received a new message from God: an order to go out and spread the word of the new faith publicly. The Prophet immediately obeyed this order and in the two years that followed he gained scores of new followers.

At first, Meccans were mostly unresponsive to Muhammad's message. He was not the first self-proclaimed prophet to start a religious movement. And living in a center of bustling commercial activity, the city's mostly pagan inhabitants were familiar with and generally accepting of the diverse religions of the region.

As time went on, however, a number of leading men in Mecca started to view Muhammad and his followers with worry and suspicion. The Muslims did not mince words about matters of faith. They insisted that the other gods worshiped at the Kaaba and elsewhere in Arabia were false. And they told people that they could not be on good terms with Allah unless they totally submitted themselves to him. Some leading Meccans feared that such aggressive preaching against older religious ideas might threaten the inflow of money they made from yearly visitors to the Kaaba. In addition, as Efraim Karsh of King's College London points out:

> Certain aspects of Muhammad's preaching, especially his emphasis on the equality of all believers, challenged long-standing social and genealogical [ancestor-related] structures of Mecca's tribal society. Besides, Arabian tradition tended to equate leadership with superior wisdom and judgment. Acceptance of Muhammad's claim to religious authority, let alone endorsement of his [growing] faith, would have amounted to acknowledgment of his political leadership, something that Mecca's elite was loath [reluctant] to do.

For these reasons, members of Mecca's ruling class began to persecute the Muslims. They also urged other people to harass and threaten them. Some of the Muslims decided to flee to what is now Ethiopia, in northeastern Africa, where sympathetic local

Christians gave them refuge. Among the approximately eighty who made the journey were Muhammad's daughter, Ruqayya, and her husband, Uthman. The Muslims who remained in Mecca, including Muhammad, did their best to withstand the cruel treatment they received in their homeland.

The Flight to Medina

The situation in Mecca for the persecuted Muslims grew increasingly worse. Both Khadija and Muhammad's uncle, Abu Talib, died in 619. Though not a Muslim convert, Abu Talib had been a widely respected and influential member of Meccan society, and he had used that influence to provide at least some measure of protection for his nephew. With his uncle gone, however, Muhammad could no longer count on such protection.

Faced with mounting death threats, the Prophet decided it was time to leave his hometown. Early in 622, he sent most of the seventy Muslims remaining in Mecca to the town of Yathrib. Located about 215 miles (350 km) north of Mecca, Yathrib soon became known as Medina (from *Medinat un-Nabi*, meaning "City of the Prophet"). Then, during the night of July 16, the last members of the group, Muhammad and Abu Bakr, departed for Medina. A group of Meccans bent on killing them gave chase, but the two men were able to elude their pursuers and reach safety. Ever after, the flight to Medina came to be called the *Hijra* (or *Hegira*; from the Arabic *hajara*, meaning "emigrate" or "depart"). It was "a watershed in Islamic history," Karsh states, "aptly designated after the Prophet's death as the official starting point of the Muslim era. At one fell swoop, Muhammad was transformed from a private preacher into a political and military leader . . . and Islam from a persecuted cult into a major religious and political force in the Arabian Peninsula."

THE MUSLIM CALENDAR

The year of the Hijra, 622, marked not only the start of the Muslim era, but also the first year of the new Muslim calendar. In that dating system, the standard Christian calendar's date of July 1, 622 CE corresponds to the first day of the month of Muharram in the year AH 1. (The letters AH stand for Anno Hijrae, or "the year of the Hijra.") One can find the roughly equivalent Muslim date of a year in the Christian calendar by subtracting 622. (For example, for Muslims the year of Christopher Columbus's first voyage—1492 CE—is 1492 minus 622, or AH 870.)

The Muslims prospered in Medina, where the town's inhabitants were more tolerant of new religious ideas. The new faith began growing by leaps and bounds, and it soon became clear that polytheism in Arabia was on the wane.

The Quba Mosque in Medina, Saudi Arabia, is the oldest mosque in the world. The Prophet Muhammad began its construction by laying its first stones down with his own hands.

A map of Saudi Arabia, featuring Medina, the second-holiest city in Islam and home to the three oldest mosques in Islam

Chapter

3

Basic Beliefs and Rituals

The period of early Islam in which Muhammad and his followers took refuge in Medina had important consequences for the fledgling faith. There, in the course of only a few years, Islam would take shape and flourish. These pioneering Muslims propelled Islam's triumph over the other belief systems in Arabia, and their example formed the basis of most of the beliefs, rituals, and customs that would later become standard for Muslims in all places and times.

The First Islamic State

One of the more important customs that Muhammad introduced while living in Medina was theocracy. A theocracy is a government or ruling council that is at least partly inspired and guided by religious beliefs and rules. Muhammad was already a religious leader when he arrived in Medina; there, he became an administrative and military leader as well. And in the centuries that followed, the notion of fusing church and state gained influence in the Islamic empires of the greater Middle East.

Muhammad did not merely advocate forming a state in which government and religion would come together for the good of the community—he actually formed such a state in Medina. Not long after the *Hijra,* he drew up what came to be called the Constitution of Medina. This charter was essentially an agreement between the families and various ethnic and interest groups making up the community (*ummah*) and that community's spiritual leader, Muhammad. The constitution provided for physical protection for all members of the *ummah*; religious freedom for Muslims, Jews, and other local groups; and payment of taxes by all to support the state.

The Prophet periodically introduced rituals and other customs that Muslims would follow ever after. In 624, for example, he changed the *qibla*, or direction a worshiper faced while praying. He had originally said that a person should face Jerusalem, since that had been the symbolic home of earlier Jewish prophets, including Abraham and Jesus. However, the *qibla* now became the location of the sacred Kaaba, which was in Mecca. (Muhammad and other Muslims believed that Abraham and his son, Ishmael, had built the Kaaba many centuries before. They also believed that Ishmael had gone on to establish the Arab race of people.)

Muhammad set another important precedent for the faithful by erecting a house in Medina. The layout and appearance of the structure was copied later when local Muslims built a mosque on the same site. Called the Prophet's Mosque, it became the second holiest Islamic shrine after the Kaaba.

UNITY WITHIN THE UMMAH

The following provisions of the Constitution of Medina stress the importance of unity among the diverse members of the community:

They [Muslims] are one community (ummah) to the exclusion of all men. . . . Believers shall not leave anyone destitute among them. . . . The God-fearing believers shall be against the rebellious or him who seeks to spread injustice, or sin, or animosity, or corruption between believers; the hand of every man shall be against him even if he be a son of one of them. . . . A believer shall not slay a believer for the sake of an unbeliever, nor shall he aid an unbeliever against a believer. . . . The peace of the believers is indivisible.

Medina and Mecca at War

Muhammad certainly directed a great deal of his attention to the Constitution of Medina and other administrative and religious duties; but he also found time to lead his followers in battle against hostile forces. Particularly unfriendly were most Meccans, including members of Muhammad's own Quraysh tribe.

The Muslims struck their first blow against the Meccans in 624. Muhammad ordered an attack on a well-guarded camel caravan that was on its way to Mecca from Syria. In what came to be known as the Battle of Badr, the Muslims, though significantly outnumbered, won.

The following year, however, the Meccans struck back and defeated Muhammad's forces in the battle of Uhud. Thinking they could now fairly easily finish off the Muslims, in 627 the Meccans marched on Medina in force. They laid siege to the town for forty days. But in an unexpected turn of events, they lost the so-called Battle of the Trench. According to scholar Karen Armstrong:

> Muhammad protected the settlement by digging a ditch around Medina, which threw the Quraysh, who . . . had never heard of such a [war tactic], into confusion, and rendered their cavalry useless. Muhammad's second victory over the numerically superior Quraysh . . . was a turning point. It convinced the nomadic tribes that Muhammad was the coming man and made the Quraysh look [outmoded]. The gods in whose name they fought were clearly not working on their behalf.

Observers from across Arabia began to suspect that Muhammad's god, Allah, might be superior to those other deities.

A painting depicting a pursuit scene from the Battle of Badr in *Jami' al-Tawarikh,* or *Universal History,* written at the start of the fourteenth century by Persian historian Rashid al-din Hamadani

Or perhaps, as Muhammad had repeatedly insisted, those traditional gods did not even exist. Taking advantage of such perceptions, the Prophet negotiated a treaty with the Meccans. In it, Mecca's leaders agreed to allow Muslims to visit and pray at the Kaaba.

Once the Islamic faithful had access to the holy city, their enemies were no longer able to counter or resist their spiritual enthusiasm. And in 629, Muhammad and his followers took Mecca without a fight. Several leading members of the Quraysh soon converted to Islam and Muhammad removed the statues of the traditional gods from the Kaaba.

The Qur'an, Angels, and Hell

Only three years after taking charge of Mecca, Muhammad died unexpectedly. The exact cause is unknown, but based on the reported symptoms—fever, headaches, muscle pains, and weakness—some specialists suggest it might have been bacterial meningitis. An infection of the fluid in the spinal cord or the fluid surrounding the brain, this disease frequently results in death.

Whatever the cause, Muhammad passed away in Medina on June 8, 632, at roughly the age of sixty-three. His followers were devastated. As historian Paul Lunde puts it, "The community had suddenly lost its Prophet, leader, friend, guide, and counselor."

Although the still relatively small Muslim community no longer had its founder, it was able to carry on and prosper without him. One main reason that Islam continued to thrive was that Muhammad had outlined in the Qur'an certain beliefs and rituals that Muslims were to follow—valuable moral and spiritual instruction and the basis of Islamic rules and legal concepts.

The Qur'an prescribed guidelines for living, worship, and organization. Muslims still believe that the volume's contents are God's literal words as passed to the Prophet by the angel Gabriel. Initially transmitted orally from person to person, these words were finally written down shortly after Muhammad's death, when his friend, Abu Bakr, governed the faithful.

The Qur'an also formulated the concept of God in his divinity and power. The following excerpt, often called the "Throne Verse," plainly and, many Muslims believe, beautifully conveys Allah's nature:

> Allah is He besides Whom there is no god, the Ever-living, the Self-subsisting by Whom all subsist; slumber does not overtake Him nor sleep; whatever is in the heavens and whatever is in the earth is His; who is he that can intercede with Him but by His permission? He knows

what is before them and what is behind them, and they cannot comprehend anything out of His knowledge except what He pleases. His knowledge extends over the heavens and the earth, and the preservation of them both tires Him not, and He is the Most High, the Great.

A Qur'an from the early twentieth century

Muslims saw (and today still see) the original Arabic version of the Qur'an as more accurate and superior to any other translation of it. God and Gabriel had delivered their messages in Arabic, so the exact meanings of the book's words and phrases can be fully understood only in that language.

Gabriel's role in giving Muhammad the Quranic text fulfills another basic Islamic precept—the belief in angels. In Arabic the word *malak,* which translates as angel, means "messenger." This is fitting, since Muslims believe that Gabriel transferred God's sacred messages to Muhammad. In Islam, angels also sing God's praises to humanity; keep track of human activities, including sins and good deeds; and guide the souls of people either to heaven or hell after death.

As regards heaven and hell, the Qur'an painted a vivid picture of both places. Similar to descriptions of hell in various Christian writings, the Qur'an made it clear that the souls of sinners would suffer in that awful place:

> [They will wear] garments of fire, [and] boiling water shall be poured over their heads. With it shall be melted what is in their bellies and their skins as well. And for them are whips of iron. Whenever they will desire to go forth from it, from grief, they shall be turned back into it, and taste the chastisement of burning.

By contrast, the righteous were destined for heaven after death: "Surely Allah will make those who [do] good deeds enter gardens beneath which rivers flow; they shall be adorned therein with bracelets of gold and with pearls, and their garments therein shall be of silk."

The Five Pillars

Among the other important Islamic beliefs and rituals that developed early in the faith's history are the so-called Five Pillars. All practicing Muslims were (and still are) expected to perform these acts. (An exception is when a person is physically unable to do so. Also, the five pillars as described here are for Sunni Muslims; Shia Muslims perform them with a few slight variations.)

The first of the Five Pillars, the *shahadah,* consists of a fundamental creed, or statement of belief. The term *shahadah* means "to bear witness;" so the person who recites it during prayer is bearing witness before God to the following oath: "I testify that there is none worthy of worship except God; Muhammad is the prophet of God." By tradition, Muslims say the *shahadah* in Arabic. Also, in order to become a Muslim, a person must recite this creed in front of two or more witnesses.

The second pillar of Islam is known as *salah* (or *salat*), which is the series of ritual prayers performed five times each day. The Qur'an stipulates that prayer should be carried out in a clean environment and that if missed, should be made up later. As originally established by Muhammad, the person praying faces in the direction of Mecca, where the Kaaba rests. The person follows tradition by going through a series of gestures and body movements, including momentarily placing his or her hands and forehead on the ground or floor.

In most Muslim countries, as well as many Muslim neighborhoods in non-Muslim nations, the faithful receive a reminder that it is time to pray. Known as the *adhan*, this call is delivered by a muezzin, an official in a local mosque. Often in musical tones, he calls out a close approximation of the following message:

"God is the most Great! I testify that there is no god but God. I testify that Muhammad is the Messenger of God. Come to prayer! Come to salvation! God is the most Great! There is no god but God!"

The third pillar, the *zakat,* is the practice of giving alms, or charity, to the poor and less fortunate in society. In non-Muslim societies, people give charitable contributions voluntarily. In Muslim cultures, however, such giving is a religious obligation, especially for those who are well off.

The fourth pillar for most Muslims is the *sawm,* in some ways similar to the Christian custom of fasting during Lent. The *sawm* consists of refraining from eating and drinking from sunup to sundown during the holy month of Ramadan. By fasting, the worshiper expresses gratefulness to God and hopes to make up for past sins. (Some Muslim groups fast at other times of the year instead of Ramadan.)

Pilgrims circling the Kaaba. Faithful Muslims circumambulate the Kaaba, or perform the ritual *Tawaf,* seven times, in a counterclockwise direction, as part of the *hajj,* the fifth pillar of Islam.

JIHAD A SIXTH PILLAR?

A few groups of Sunni Muslims recognize a sixth pillar of the faith, namely Jihad. Its literal meaning is translated simply as "to strive" or "to struggle" and as a concept it is interpreted as "striving for the cause, or way, of Allah." Jihad can mean struggle in the sense of pursuing a worthy cause. And in that sense it can be a personal struggle, such as striving to achieve moral excellence. It can also be defined as a social struggle for a just cause, such as religious freedom that has been lost. Jihad can also refer to warfare. In this context it most often consists of defending Islamic lands or rights. Only rarely has it applied to offensive conflicts, the so-called "holy wars" frequently portrayed in Western media.

The last of the traditional five pillars is the *hajj*, or journey to Mecca. Every Muslim who is physically and financially able to do so is expected to fulfill this duty at least once in his or her lifetime. Reaching the holy city, pilgrims walk seven times around the Kaaba, as well as visit other sacred sites in Mecca.

Like other basic concepts and rituals of Islamic worship, the *hajj* and other pillars have changed hardly at all over time. Once established in the faith's early centuries, they have remained strong bastions of tradition. "Now, as in the past," says British professor of religion Neal Robinson, those who perform the *hajj* and other basic acts of the faith feel "fully integrated into the worldwide community of Muslims."

The interior of the
Cathedral and former
Great Mosque of
Córdoba, Spain

Chapter

4

The Early Caliphs and Expansion

When Muhammad passed away in 632 CE, at first no one was certain who should or would take his place as Islam's leader. Many years after his death, competing Muslim groups would claim to know whom the Prophet intended as his successor. One of these groups, the Shia, came to believe that Muhammad wanted his cousin and son-in-law, Ali, to take his place. The faith's leader, the Shia contended, should be a descendant of Muhammad through his kinsman Ali. Another major group, the Sunnis, disagreed. They came to believe that any successor chosen through consensus among the *ummah* is the legitimate leader. Still other scholars suggest that it remains unclear what Muhammad's intentions about succession really were. For example, British-born Lesley Hazleton, a veteran Middle East journalist, writes:

> In everything that was to follow [Muhammad's death], everyone claimed to have insight into what the Prophet thought and what he wanted. Yet in the lack of a clear and unequivocal [undisputed] designation of his successor, nobody could prove it beyond any shadow of a doubt. However convinced they may have been that they were right, there were always those who would maintain otherwise. Certainty was a matter of faith rather than fact.

DISPUTED WORDS BY THE PROPHET

Most Shia scholars believe that Muhammad said the following words shortly before his death. Many Sunni scholars, on the other hand, dispute this version of the story, saying that these words were likely added later.

> *The time approaches when I shall be called away by God and I shall answer that call. I am leaving you with two precious things and if you adhere to both of them, you will never go astray. They are the Quran, the Book of God, and my family. . . . The two shall never separate from each other until they come to me by the pool of Paradise.*

Whatever Muhammad's actual intentions about his successor may have been, shortly after his passing his chief advisors and closest friends chose that successor: Abu Bakr, the man who fled with Muhammad from Mecca to Medina in 622. Bakr was not only a close and loyal friend; he was also Muhammad's father-in-law because Bakr's daughter, Aisha, had married the Prophet in 623.

As the new leader of the faith and the Muslim community, Bakr was given the title of caliph (from the Arabic word *khalifa*, meaning "deputy"). Bakr became known to future Muslims as one of a group of early Islamic leaders called the "Rightly Guided Caliphs." The first three of these deputies, beginning with Bakr, presided over an enormous and unprecedented expansion of Arab-Muslim-controlled territory. An Islamic empire, often called the caliphate, emerged under their rule, marking the first time in history that an Arab state became a world power.

Bakr's Audacious Vision

Bakr had been caliph only a few weeks when he faced his first major crisis. In the last few years before his death, Muhammad had brought nearly all the tribes in Arabia into the Muslim fold—including most of the nomadic Bedouins. Now that the Prophet was gone, however, a majority of the Bedouins decided that they owed no allegiance to his successor. Their rebellion against the Islamic community became known as the *Ridda*. Bakr managed to prove himself a strong leader by attacking and defeating the Bedouins in a series of small-scale battles. In less than a year, the revolt collapsed and Arabia was once more united under a single Muslim leader.

Yet Bakr and his advisors worried that more threats to the *ummah* might materialize in the future. Moreover, some of these threats might well come from outside the Arabian peninsula. Of particular concern were the two large empires that controlled much of the Middle East—the Sassanian and Byzantine realms. One or both of them might see the newly unified Arabia as a potential danger to their own interests, and that might lead them to attack Arab lands.

This reasoning was almost certainly what in part led Bakr to preempt an attack on Arabia by striking first against his rivals. He ordered raids into Iraq and Palestine in 633. The towns that surrendered to the Arabs during these operations lay on the fringes of Sassanian and Byzantine territories, and these nations could be expected to retaliate. Many non-Arabs likely viewed Bakr's provoking these powerful empires as an audacious or even foolhardy move.

Yet Bakr and his advisors apparently considered that they possessed two significant advantages. First, Sassanian and Byzantine forces in the region were not very well organized and had the bulk of their energies focused on fighting each other. Second, the Arabs felt they had a worthy and just cause to fight for. Muhammad had convinced them that they had a right to struggle against unbelievers who might pose a threat to the Islamic community. "This vision," Efraim Karsh explains, "together with Islam's unwavering feeling of supremacy and buoyant conviction in its ultimate triumph, imbued [filled] the early believers with the necessary sense of purpose, self-confidence, and revolutionary zeal to take on the region's established empires."

A late-medieval Muslim historian, Abdel Rahman ibn Khaldun, described that singular, remarkable zeal this way: "When people possess the [correct] insight into their affairs, nothing can withstand them, because their outlook is one [and the same] and they share a unity of purpose for which they are willing to die."

A watch tower in the Hajar Mountains, near the four hundred-year-old town of Al Hamra, Oman, on the Arabian Peninsula

Umar's Wise Decisions

Bakr did not live long enough to see the full-scale wars with the Byzantines and Sassanians come to pass. He died in August 634 after serving as caliph for only two years. Before he passed away, however, he named his successor—Umar ibn al-Khattab, another of Muhammad's close friends and fathers-in-law. Umar proved to be an ambitious and vigorous military leader. He carried on and greatly expanded the attacks that Bakr had initiated in regions claimed by the Byzantines and Sassanians. Between 634 and 642, Arab forces overran Palestine, including its major city of Jerusalem; they took Syria, including the large city of Damascus, along with Egypt, from the Byzantines; and they wrested Iraq (then called Mesopotamia) from the Sassanians. These successes in large part came about because of the skills and sheer brilliance of the Muslim military general Khalid ibn al-Walid.

THE BATTLE OF AL-YARMOUK

One of the key events in the Arab capture of Syria was the Battle of Yarmouk, fought in 636. An Arab chronicler named Al-Baladhuri wrote this account of the battle some two centuries after it occurred.

Beyond the ravines lies the area in which the Battle of Yarmouk took place.

[The Byzantine emperor] Heraclius gathered large bodies of Greeks, Syrians, Mesopotamians, and Armenians numbering about 200,000 . . . resolving to fight the *[invading Arabs]. The Muslims gathered together and the [Byzantine] army marched against them. The battle they fought at al-Yarmouk was of the fiercest and bloodiest kind. . . . The [Byzantines] and their followers in this battle tied themselves to each other by chains, so that no one might set his hope on flight. . . . Some 70,000 of them [died] and their remnants took to flight, reaching as far as Palestine . . . Mesopotamia, and Armenia.*

During these military campaigns, Umar made some important and wise administrative decisions. These choices both shaped the destiny of the conquered lands for subsequent generations and helped ensure that the Muslim expansion begun by Muhammad and Bakr would continue. One of Umar's decisions regarded the fate of the territories the Muslims had overrun. A common tradition in ancient and medieval times was for military victors to divide up conquered lands among themselves. But Umar forbade this. "Allah has made those who come after you partners in these spoils," he announced. "Were I to divide these lands among you, nothing will be left for them."

Instead, the Arab and Muslim soldiers were ordered to remain in special military camps and were not allowed to settle down as farmers and merchants. This mandate had enormous consequences. First, the conquered peoples were allowed to retain most of their lands, along with their native cultures—making them less likely to rebel against their new rulers. Second, as University of Cambridge scholar Patricia Crone points out, "Without [Umar's approach], the Arabs might have dispersed as landlords and peasants among the conquered peoples, who would rapidly have absorbed them." Because this did not happen, Umar and his successor retained large, battle-hardened military forces with which to carry on their conquests.

Another important policy established during early Arab expansion involved the religious beliefs of the defeated peoples. The new

Islamic rulers of the conquered lands maintained an attitude of religious tolerance toward Christians, Jews, and other non-Muslim residents. According to Karen Armstrong, author of *Muhammad* and *Islam: A Short History*:

> There was nothing religious about these campaigns, and Umar did not believe that he had a divine mandate to conquer the world. The objective of Umar and his warriors was entirely pragmatic [practical]: they wanted plunder and a common activity that would preserve the unity of the ummah. . . . Furthermore, once the Arabs had left the peninsula, they found that nearly everybody belonged to [the] People of the Book, who had received authentic scriptures from God. They were not, therefore, forced to convert to Islam. Indeed, until the middle of the eighth century, conversion was not encouraged.

The Reign of Uthman

Despite Umar's remarkable statesmanship as ruler of the conquered peoples, his administrators sometimes encountered resentment and resistance. Local opposition was most pronounced in Persia, where tensions came to a head in 644. A Persian prisoner of war who had been taken to Medina managed to get close enough to Umar to fatally stab him. On his deathbed, the caliph urged six high-ranking Arab-Muslim leaders to choose his successor.

This committee chose Uthman ibn Affan. In addition to being Muhammad's son-in-law, he had the further distinction of having been the fourth male convert to Islam. The new caliph did not expand the empire as much as Umar had. Nevertheless, the new territories that Uthman acquired were considerable. He captured the large eastern Mediterranean island of Cyprus, which had been ruled by the Byzantines; his armies moved westward from Egypt into what is now Libya; and in the east, the Caliphate absorbed significant pieces of Armenia, Iran, and Afghanistan. Uthman also ordered the building of the first-ever Arab-Muslim naval force. The fleet roamed the waters near Cyprus, Palestine, and Egypt, keeping the Byzantines from recapturing the lands they had recently lost to the Arabs.

Another of the third caliph's noteworthy achievements was his ordering the creation of a definitive, or perfect and authoritative, text of the Qur'an. By the time of his reign, various dialects of Arabic were developing across the growing empire. Readings of the holy book had begun to differ slightly from one another, and changes had begun to creep into the text. From one of Muhammad's surviving wives, Uthman acquired a copy of the original manuscript, which was written in the dialect of the Prophet's own tribe, the Quraysh. That copy became the model for a new set of copies produced by Uthman's scholars and scribes. All variant versions of the Qur'an were destroyed. In this way, a version almost identical to the one initially introduced by Muhammad was preserved for future generations.

Uthman had intended the production of an authoritative version of the Qur'an to be a unifying act that would please all Muslims. Yet a great deal of discontent developed during his reign, especially among soldiers and administrators in the conquered lands. Many of these men accused Uthman of showing too much favoritism to men from his own clan, the Umayya. In 656, several army veterans who felt this way traveled to Medina to lodge a protest. When the caliph refused to give in to their demands, they killed him. This unexpected and violent act threw the new Islamic empire into disarray. A civil war erupted and for the first time the strong, monolithic Muslim community that Muhammad had forged began to fracture and fragment.

A mosque at dusk

Chapter

5

Divisions
Among the
Faithful

The divisions and strife that rocked the Muslim community following Uthman's death had several dimensions. On the one hand what erupted was a family feud over the position of caliph. Muhammad's cousin and son-in-law Ali had been passed over for that high-ranking post three times in a row, as Bakr, Umar, and Uthman had all had their turns as leader of the *ummah*. Now, Ali and his followers felt it was only right for him to have *his* turn. After all, they said, the Prophet had held Ali in high esteem, saying: "I am the City of Knowledge and Ali is its gateway."

Opposing Ali for the position of caliph was Muawiya ibn Abi Sufian (or Sufyan). Muawiya was Uthman's cousin and another leading member of the Umayyad clan, as well as governor of Syria under Uthman. Also against Ali were one of Muhammad's widows, Aisha, and two of her prominent kinsmen, Talhah and Zubayr.

At the root of the debate, however, was a fundamental question: what determines succession to the caliphate? This issue had divided not only those prominent families mentioned above—it had divided all Muslims, mostly into two groups. One group felt that a relative of the Prophet should rule the *ummah*. The other group believed that the worthiest person should rule, whether a relative or not.

The civil war that erupted in the wake of Uthman's assassination greatly intensified this disagreement, and members of the former group backed Ali, while members of the latter backed Muawiya. This controversy marked the beginning of the major split between Shia Muslims and Sunni Muslims. Moreover, as the war dragged on, there also emerged a group of believers who felt that neither Ali nor Muawiya should rule. Many of the faithful worried that these divisions would make it difficult to restore the unity that had once existed among them. And in retrospect, they were right.

Attempts at Negotiation

Three major events precipitated the fragmentation of the original *ummah*. The first was Uthman's murder. The second was Ali's acceptance of the office of caliph, which several leading Muslims of Medina had offered him. He established his capital at Kufa, in southern Iraq. Although Uthman's violent death had shocked him as much as anyone else, he made no immediate attempt to

A painting of Ali ibn Abi Talib, Muhammad's cousin, by Ahmad Reza Haraji

find the assassins. His apparent indifference was likely due to the fact that large numbers of Ali's followers—his political base, so to speak—felt that Uthman had been neither a good ruler nor a good Muslim. So, they said, he deserved to be killed. The third event that ensured Muslim unity would crumble was Muawiya's announcement that he opposed Ali. Muawiya criticized Ali's failure to go after the assassins and challenged him for the position of caliph.

Before Ali could muster his forces to meet that challenge, however, he first had to deal with his other leading opponents, Aisha, Talhah, and Zubayr. The latter two, Aisha's brothers-in-law, had at first given their allegiance to Ali. But Aisha was able to persuade them to switch their loyalties to her. From Ali's viewpoint, since these three opposed the sitting caliph, they were rebels against the Muslim state.

These so-called rebels hastily gathered their local supporters, probably numbering about a thousand, and late in 656 marched northward from Mecca. Over the course of a few weeks, their numbers grew to 3,000 or more. When Ali learned of this mounting opposition, he at first refused to move against the rebels—perhaps he was hoping they would change their minds and disperse, and if so, preserve the unity of the Islamic community.

The new caliph soon found, however, that Aisha and her supporters had marched northward to Basra, southeast of Kufa in southern Iraq. It appeared they planned to make that important city their base and from it march on Kufa. Ali speedily assembled as many soldiers as he could find and led them to Basra. Hoping to settle the dispute by negotiations, he met with Talhah and Zubayr. These talks went on for most of the day, and it appears that both parties agreed to continue them the next day.

The Battle of the Camel

The talks did not bring about a peaceful solution. The next morning, while it was still dark, fighting broke out between the opposing forces. Each side was under the impression that the other was the aggressor. To this day no one knows for sure who actually struck first. As political journalist Hazleton explains:

> The accounts are confused, as battle accounts always are. A small group, certainly [was responsible], but [even] the smallest group can set huge armies into motion. Three or four men can do it easily. The clanging of steel rises from a single sector, curses and battle cries carry through the still air of early morning, and suddenly thousands are involved. In the terror and desperation of battle, there is no time for questions. Who struck the first blow is the last thing on anyone's mind as every man fights for his life.

Ultimately, it mattered little who had struck the first blow. Not long after the sun had risen, both armies were fully engaged in battle. They fought for hours and eventually the tide of battle shifted near the litter in which Aisha was sitting. When she had become surrounded, her soldiers gathered around the litter and the camel that pulled it, hoping to protect her. One of them held the camel's reins with one hand and her battle standard with the other. When he was struck down, another took his place. And so it went, warrior after warrior, until seventy men in a row had stood by the camel and fallen to their deaths. (For this reason, the conflict later became popularly known as the Battle of the Camel, although it is also called the Battle of Basra.)

Finally, Ali put a stop to the carnage. He ordered one of his own men to cut the beast's hamstrings, which would bring it down. The wounded camel let out a loud bellow and collapsed into a heap, after which the fighting stopped. It soon became clear that Aisha had survived the battle, although she had been hit in the arm by an arrow. Ali checked to make sure she was not seriously hurt, for the last thing he wanted was for one of the widows of his beloved kinsman Muhammad to be killed. Ali made sure that Aisha was taken into the city and treated with kindness and respect, despite her attempted rebellion.

The victor also inspected the battlefield and found that several thousand men, mostly members of the rebel forces, had been slain. (The exact casualty figures, like the sizes of the opposing forces, are unknown.) Among the dead were Talhah and Zubayr. Actually, the number of rebel dead might have been much higher,

but Ali had given orders to his officers that any rebels who fled the field were not to be pursued. Nor were any wounded rebels to be killed, nor any of their valuables to be seized. His lenience in these respects was likely part of an effort to minimize the killing of Muslims by other Muslims. Also, it may be that he wanted to establish himself as a man of mercy and forgiveness who planned to govern all Muslims fairly. A letter he wrote to one of his officials (an administrator who was about to take charge of Egypt) provides insight into the kind of man he was and leader he hoped to be:

> You must create in your mind kindness, compassion and love for your subjects. Do not behave towards them as if you are a voracious and ravenous beast and as if your success lies in devouring them. Remember [that your

subjects] are human beings like you. . . . They commit sins, indulge in vices either intentionally [or] unintentionally without realizing the enormity of their deeds. Let your mercy and compassion come to their rescue and help in the same way and to the same extent that you expect Allah to show mercy and forgiveness to you.

Showdown at Siffin

Soon after his win at Basra, Ali also attempted to negotiate with his chief rival, Muawiya. But the latter refused to serve under Ali and insisted on ruling Syria and its surrounding territories as a caliph in his own right. Once more, war seemed the only realistic solution. And in 657 the opposing armies gathered at Siffin, near the border between Syria and Iraq.

ALI APPEALS TO ALLAH

Before the onset of fighting at Siffin, witnesses claimed that Ali appealed to God to grant him and his followers victory:

O my Allah! Sustainer of the high sky and the suspended firmament which you have made a shelter for the night and the day, an orbit for the sun and the moon, and a path for the rotating stars. . . . If you give us victory over our enemy, [we ask that you] save us from excesses and keep us on the straight path of truth. But if you give them victory over us, then grant us martyrdom and save us from mischief.

The clash at Siffin was a long, drawn-out affair. Fighting raged on and off for days with both sides suffering considerable losses. Eventually, the two commanders agreed to allow a tribunal, or panel, of devout Muslims to decide which man had the more acceptable claim to the office of caliph. Both Ali and Muawiya said they would support the tribunal's verdict.

But the fact that Ali had agreed to arbitrate matters only further angered a small group of his devout and more radical supporters. In Karen Armstrong's words,

> [they] refused to accept the arbitration and were shocked by Ali's submission. In their view . . . Ali had compromised with the supporters of injustice by failing to right the wrongs committed by Uthman and was, therefore, no true Muslim. They withdrew from the ummah, which they claimed had betrayed the spirit of the Quran, and set up their own camp with an independent commander.

These separatists later came to be called the Kharijites, or "those who went out" (from the Arabic *khariji*, meaning "one who departs" or "dissenter"). Ali felt he could not allow them to undermine his own cause. So he gathered his other supporters and fought them in 658 at Nahrawan (not far from present-day Baghdad). Although Ali decisively defeated the Kharijites, some of them survived and continued to oppose both him and Muawiya.

THE PURIST KHARIJITES

The civil war that erupted among Muslims in 656 CE brought about the emergence of a new Islamic faction known as the Kharijites. Although they started out as Ali's followers, they turned on him when he tried to negotiate with his enemy, Muawiya. The Kharijites were zealous believers in Islamic principles. And they felt that they must preserve what they saw as the faith's original purity. Well after the era of Ali, they continued to oppose a long succession of caliphs whom they considered too liberal and not devout enough. Descendants of the Kharijites still exist today. Living mainly in Oman (in southeastern Arabia) and North Africa, they reject the term Kharijite and instead call themselves Ibadi. They remain separate from and more conservative than both Sunni and Shia Muslims.

In spite of Ali's struggle with the Kharijites, he never did agree to the arbitration they so roundly condemned. The tribunal eventually ruled that he and Muawiya should both give up their efforts to become caliph. But both men ignored the panel's judgment and refused to abandon their claims to rule. Ali remained caliph in Kufa; and in 660, in Jerusalem, Muawiya declared himself caliph, too.

Meanwhile, the Kharijites secretly plotted to murder both caliphs and elect one of their own number as supreme leader. They managed to kill Ali in 661. But they were unable to get close enough to Muawiya. With Ali gone, Muawiya no longer had any credible opposition and he established the first Islamic dynasty (family line of rulers)—the Umayyads.

Although the empire once more had only one caliph, it was never again completely united. The division between Sunni and Shia was too entrenched in the minds of Muslims, and this chasm became permanent. The Shia did not recognize the authority of the Umayyads and continued to insist that only the successors of Ali, whom they called Imams, were the true leaders of the faith. The Umayyads did not like their unrelenting opponents, but they and their descendants found that it was a reality they would have to learn to deal with.

The holy Shiite shrine of Alī ibn Abī Tālib, the cousin and son-in-law of the Prophet Muhammad, whom the Shia consider to be the righteous caliph and first imam. The shrine, renowned as the site of the tomb of Ali, is located in Najaf, Iraq.

Umayyad Palace at the Citadel in Amman, Jordan

Chapter

6

Rise and Fall
of the
Umayyads

Muawiya, of the Umayyad clan, turned out to be the first of fourteen successive rulers of his family line. The dynasty—the first to oversee the Islamic realm—lasted from 661 to 750. By placing relatives in the post of caliph, the Umayyads eliminated much of the strife that had plagued the succession during the reigns of the first four caliphs.

The Umayyads also greatly expanded the pomp, ceremony, and luxury of the caliphate. Muawiya made his capital at Damascus, a sprawling, bustling Syrian city. He and his successors erected palaces for themselves and their families. They lived like kings, even though most Arabs and Muslims rejected the concept of kingship. Many later Muslim historians were critical of the Umayyads, saying that they were too concerned with their own comforts.

The Umayyads were not, however, so preoccupied with living well that they failed to accomplish much. In fact, several members of the dynasty achieved great successes both at home and abroad. On the foreign front, they commanded conquests that brought many new territories into the empire, including huge tracts of central Asia, northern Africa, and southwestern Europe.

On the domestic front, meanwhile, the Umayyads managed to maintain the general unity of the *ummah*. In the face of considerable opposition, this was no easy task. There was growing discontent from a new and rapidly expanding group known as the *mawali*, who were non-Arab converts to Islam, including large numbers of native Persians and North Africans. These new believers felt that Muslims of Arab descent were too much of a privileged class, and that members of that upper class discriminated against them socially and economically. In addition, the Umayyads still had to reckon with the Shia and Kharijites, who remained hostile toward the caliphs in Damascus.

Yazid's Challenges

The first major crisis brought about by these opposition groups occurred in 680. Following Muawiya's death, the Shia refused to accept his son Yazid as caliph. They believed that someone related to Muhammad should rule instead and declared that Ali's son, and the Prophet's grandson, Hussein (or Husain), should be elected caliph. In order to defend their claim to power Yazid and his supporters organized an offensive strike. A contingent of soldiers led by one of Yazid's commanders attacked Hussein and a small group of his own supporters at Karbala, in central Iraq. "After a short battle," describes Karsh, "Hussein fled to the small town of Karbala, where he soon found himself under siege. [Yazid's commander] called upon him to surrender, but Hussein . . . remained defiant. He was killed in the ensuing battle, on October 10, 680, and his head was sent on a platter to Damascus after being paraded [by Yazid's soldiers] in Kufa. Hussein's death was to prove a watershed in the history of Islam [because] it helped cement the [Shia] into a significant and cohesive [solid] religious movement."

"EVERY PLACE IS KARBALA"

University of Calgary scholar Erica Fraser explains the significance of Hussein's defeat at Karbala for future generations of Shia.

The killing of the Prophet's grandson horrified all Muslims, but Shia were particularly affected. For them, Karbala marked the final division between Shia and Sunni Islam, and Hussein forever became a martyr for Shiism. The battle, which in the Muslim calendar occurred in the month of Muharram, is commemorated every year by Shia to this day. Clay from Karbala is often pressed into tablets for Shia around the world to use in their prayers. Iran's late Ayatollah Khomeini often used the phrase, "Every day is Muharram, every place is Karbala," to inspire Iran's mostly Shia population.

Challenges to Yazid's position as caliph did not end with Hussein's death. An Arab named Abdullah ibn Zubayr launched the next rebellion in 683 and Yazid responded by sending an army into Arabia. That army captured Medina and then assaulted Mecca, where many of Zubayr's followers had gathered. The fighting was so intense that the holy Kaaba caught fire; but suddenly news arrived that Yazid had died unexpectedly and the battle ended.

A New Wave of Expansion

Yazid, whose caliphate had been brief, was succeeded by two other short-lived Umayyad rulers, Muawiya II and Marwan I. The first member of the dynasty to have a long reign was Abd al-Malik. After coming to power in 685, he vigorously pursued a series of important domestic programs. One was the creation of an administrative system similar to that of the Byzantines, with government departments, each headed by a public official.

Al-Malik also introduced reforms designed to make the Arab-ruled empire more Arab, at least in appearance. He hoped that if the government set an example, Arab culture and customs might more easily take hold among the realm's masses of non-Arabs. His first action in pursuit of this goal was to ban the use of Persian and Greek in government and make Arabic the official language. According to Richard Hooker:

> Islam was [very] closely connected with being Arab, [and] being Arab, of course, was more than an ethnic identity, it was a tribal identity based on kinship and descent. As more and more Muslims were non-Arabs, the status of Arabs and their culture became threatened. In particular, large numbers of Coptic-speaking

[Egyptian] and Persian-speaking Muslims threatened the primacy of the very language that Islam is based on.

Al-Malik also promoted and bolstered Arab identity and culture by issuing the first Islamic coinage. (The Muslims had used coins before, but they had featured mainly Christian and Zoroastrian symbols. The new coins were stamped with Arabic words and symbols.)

Another of al-Malik's major achievements was a series of Islamic conquests that served to expand the empire. In the east, Muslim armies pushed northeastward from Iran and Afghanistan and neared the borders of China. Even more extensive were his campaigns in the west. At the time, the Arabic word for west, *Maghrib,* referred more specifically to coastal North Africa, then ruled by the Byzantines. Al-Malik's armies overran Libya between 663 and 666. And what is now Tunisia fell to the Muslims by 670. The wave of expansion continued, and by the end of al-Malik's reign in 705, it had reached the shores of the Atlantic Ocean.

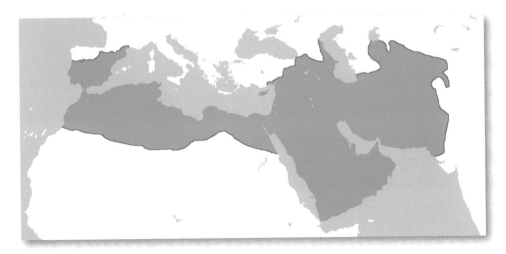

A map featuring the Umayyad Caliphate during its peak, circa 750 CE. The map is partially based on a world map of the period 500 to 750 CE in the 2007 *Atlas of World History.*

The Muslim campaigns did not stop with al-Malik's passing. Under his successor, al-Walid, in 711 Umayyad forces began crossing the Strait of Gibraltar into what is now Spain. At the time Spain was under the sway of a tribal people called the Visigoths, who were Christians. The invading Umayyads soundly defeated the Visigoths and seized all of Spain except its north-ernmost reaches.

FIGHTING FOR A CAUSE

Scholars and others have long debated how the Arab-Muslim armies were able to conquer so much territory in only a few decades. Their success was at least partially the result of effective fighting skills and leadership. But as military historian Christon Archer points out, even more decisive was high morale and belief in their cause:

The Arabs [were successful] partly through an aggressive and demanding religion and partly through the economic and political rewards that successful expansion brought. The previous feuding of Arab tribes was channeled into a communal obligation to perform jihad, or holy war, not to convert unbelievers, but to achieve the universal domination of Islam. All of this obviously created a series of armies that had considerable incentives to succeed.

Seven years later, in 718, a Muslim army under the Umayyad caliph Umar II crossed the Pyrenees Mountains at Spain's northern border. That provided access to what is now France, then occupied by the Franks. (Originally a Germanic tribal people, the Franks first settled in the land later named for them—France—in the fourth century.) Led by Abd ar-Rahnan al Ghafiqi, the Muslims steadily made gains in France, and by 725, during the reign of the Umayyad ruler Hisham, they had taken Autun, a town lying two hundred miles southeast of Paris. In the following year they captured Nimes, near France's Mediterranean coast. The Umayyad armies were seemingly unstoppable and braced to seize the rest of France and penetrate further into Europe.

The Muslim Advance Blocked

Up until that time, the Franks had been unable to mount an effective offensive against the invaders. In 732, however, a capable Frankish chieftain named Charles Martel put together a coalition of Franks and Burgundians. (The Burgundians were Germanic tribesmen who dwelled to the east of the Frankish lands.) This hastily assembled force moved to block the Muslim advance in west-central France. The ensuing engagement, one of the most pivotal in European history, is alternately referred to as the Battle of Poitiers and the Battle of Tours.

Surviving evidence for the battle itself is scant at best. One of several French versions, which cannot be verified, is that Martel ordered his soldiers to form a large square. Supposedly their opponents launched numerous frontal attacks on the square. But they could not fracture it. A surviving Arab account gives a bit more detail, including what happened to the Muslim commander:

The Moslem horsemen dashed fierce and frequent forward against the battalions of the Franks, who resisted manfully, and many fell dead on either side, until the going-down of the sun. . . . While Abd ar-Rahman strove to [rally his troops] the warriors of the Franks came around him, and he was pierced through with many spears, so that he died. Then all the [Muslim] host fled before the enemy, and many died in the flight.

Charles Martel (mounted) facing Abd ar-Rahman (right) at the Battle of Tours, as depicted in an oil painting by Charles de Steuben, circa the mid-1830s

After the death of Abd ar-Rahnan, his forces lost their momentum and returned to Spain to regroup. Smaller incursions of Muslim troops into southern France continued from time to time in the years that followed, but they never again managed to mount the large-scale offensive needed to take control of any more of Europe.

The Dynasty's Demise

The failure to capture more of Europe did not in any way diminish the Umayyads' military accomplishments. Overall, their expansion of the empire and *ummah* had been successful and impressive. However, in retrospect it is clear that this phenomenally rapid increase in the size of the realm had certain drawbacks.

One important shortcoming was that it was extremely difficult to manage and rule so many far-flung regions and peoples. Most of these peoples were non-Arab, and because they often suffered from discrimination, they sometimes rebelled against the Arab ruling class. In 739, for example, many North African *mawali* (mostly members of an indigenous people, the Berbers) launched a bloody revolt. It took three years for the caliph's soldiers to crush the insurrection. Moreover, the government had to deal with mounting discontent among *mawali* in Persia and elsewhere.

One Umayyad ruler made a wise and valiant attempt to redress the grievances of the *mawali* and to curb the threat they posed to the state. Umar II instituted reforms that called for granting full equality to non-Arabs. This included giving the same pensions to non-Arab army veterans as were furnished to Arab veterans. However, "these reforms," one scholar points out, "came too late to stop the tide of discontent that was sweeping the empire. Umar II died after a reign of only three years [717–720], before his thoughtful and wide-ranging reforms could take effect."

In addition to opposition from the *mawali,* the Umayyads increasingly faced protests from other groups within the realm. The Kharijites continued to challenge the authority of the rulers. And more and more ordinary Arabs complained that they lived in poverty while the caliphs and their families enjoyed lavish lifestyles.

The Shia, too, remained opposed to the Umayyads and eventually began plotting their overthrow. In 747 some Shia organized members of their own ranks, along with members of other groups opposed to the rulers. They launched a rebellion with the aim of overthrowing the Umayyad caliph and installing Abbas, a descendent of Muhammad's uncle. Abbas became the namesake for these rebels, who called themselves the Abbasids.

The Umayyads and Abbasids fought a number of battles until the rebels finally prevailed in 750. The last Umayyad caliph, Marwan II, suffered a decisive defeat near the Zab River, in Iraq. He managed to escape and flee to Egypt. But the Abbasids hunted him down and killed him, a fate subsequently met by nearly every member of the huge Umayyad family. (The only known survivor was Prince Abd al-Rahman. He went to Spain and there established the Spanish Umayyad dynasty.)

In ousting the Umayyad dynasty the Abbasids established a new Islamic Caliphate of the empire. At the time, no one could foresee that this bloodbath and the chaos surrounding it were the prelude to Islam's greatest era of achievement—the Golden Age.

The Dome of the Eagle at the Umayyad Mosque in Damascus, Syria.
The mosque is the fourth-holiest place in Islam.

The Abbasid palace of Ukhaidir,
built in the late eighth century
and located in the Iraqi Desert

Chapter

7

The Abbasids and Golden Age

When he took power in 750, the first Abbasid caliph, al-Saffah, no doubt hoped his own dynasty would last longer than that of the Umayyads. This hope was fulfilled—the Abbasids ruled for more than five centuries.

Those centuries witnessed not only relatively few episodes of war and bloodshed, but also an extraordinary flowering of the arts, literature, and science. Middle East historian Efraim Karsh calls it "one of the most momentous intellectual awakenings in world history, encompassing most spheres of intellectual and scientific activity, from astronomy, theology, philosophy, and medicine, to history, literature, and poetry." In many ways, it could be argued that the reign of the Abbasids marked the height of early Islam. In the span of a little more than six centuries, Islamic civilization had risen from extremely humble beginnings in Arabia to become a dominant force in the known world.

The Abbasid Government

The Abbasid Dynasty featured a succession of thirty-seven caliphs. Under their rule the office of caliph was very different than it had been under the Umayyads. During the Umayyad years, the caliphs were king-like heads of state who did not always live by strict Islamic standards. In contrast, the Abbasids interpreted Islamic concepts and laws in an exacting manner. They saw themselves as Allah's "shadows" on Earth. An executioner accompanied each Abbasid ruler in public, meant as a stern reminder that the caliph possessed the power of life and death over his subjects. Such public appearances were few, however. The Abbasids remained insulated from ordinary Muslims and went out in public only a few times a year.

The rest of the time, the caliphs withdrew into a walled, well-guarded inner sanctum at the core of their capital. After their victory over the Umayyads they had abandoned the previous seat of government in Syria and erected a new one—Baghdad, in south-central Iraq, which officially became the capital in 763. Writes Lunde, author of *Islam: Faith, Culture, History*:

> The core of the city, housing the caliph, was laid out according to cosmological [planetary] principles, probably of Persian origin. It was circular, with concentric circuits of walls marking off the different quarters. In the

center was the caliph's palace. The walls were pierced by four gates, oriented to the four points of the compass. Beyond the outer wall of [this so-called] Round City, suburbs grew up, and Baghdad shortly became one of the largest cities in the world.

AN EYEWITNESS TO ABBASID BAGHDAD

A Muslim writer penned this description of Baghdad at the height of Abbasid rule, around 1000 CE:

The city of Baghdad formed two vast semi-circles on the right and left banks of the Tigris [River], twelve miles in diameter. The numerous suburbs, covered with parks, gardens, villas and beautiful promenades [walkways], and plentifully supplied with rich bazaars [markets], and finely built mosques and baths, stretched for a considerable distance on both sides of the river. In the days of its prosperity the population of Baghdad and its suburbs amounted to over two millions! . . . Immense streets, none less than forty cubits [sixty-six feet] wide, traversed the city from one end to the other, dividing it into blocks.

In keeping with their withdrawal from public affairs, the Abbasid caliphs turned the actual running of the government over to an official called the *wazir* (which later became *vizier* in English). The *wazir* was a non-Arab because the caliphs wanted to emphasize that everyone, Arabs and non-Arabs alike, would be treated equally. This policy more or less eliminated the old grievances of the *mawali*.

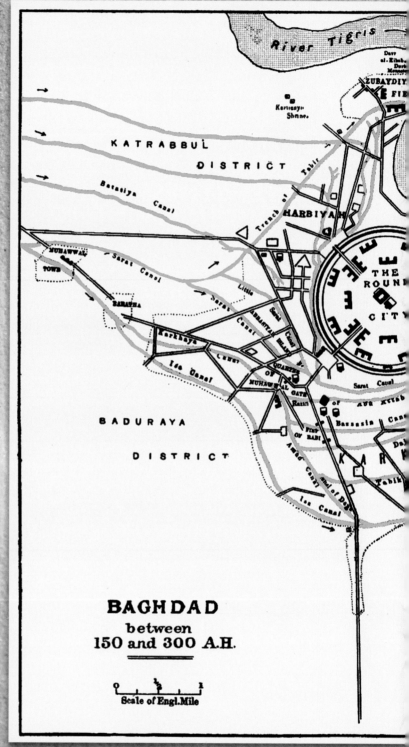

An 1883 map by William Muir depicting the city of Baghdad between 767 and 912 CE

BAGHDAD
between
150 and 300 A.H.

Scale of Engl. Mile

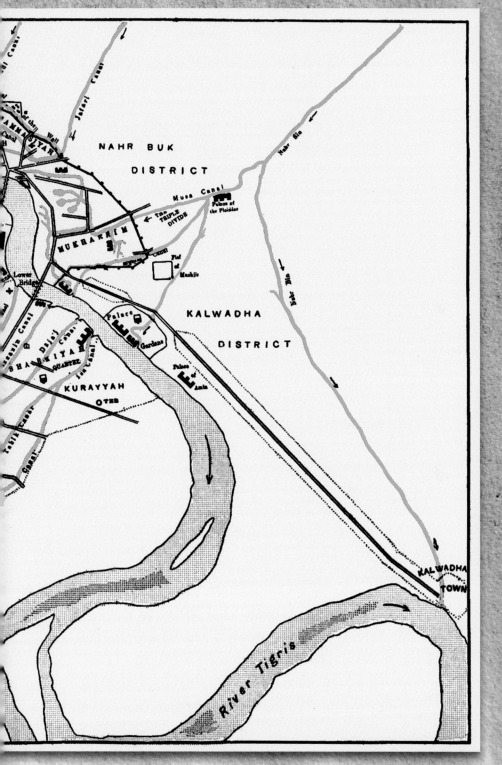

NAHR BUK
DISTRICT

Jafari Canal

Musa Canal

Nahr Bin

Palace of
the Ploiâdes

Nahr Bin

THE
TRIPLE
DIVIDE

MUKHARRIM

Plot
of
Mashjir

Lower
Bridge

Palace

KALWADHA

DISTRICT

Gardens

SHARKIYAH

QUARTER

Palace
of
Amin

KURAYYAH
OTES

KALWADHA

TOWN

River Tigris

The *wazir* was assisted in government administration by a group of literate clerks known as the *kuttab*. They helped the *wazir* run the bureaucracy's various departments. Because they could read and write and most other citizens could not, over time the *kuttab* became a privileged class; and many young men who wanted to get ahead in life sought to join their ranks.

Assistants to the *wazir* aided in coordinating the postal, or messenger, service that had been founded by the Umayyads. Under the Abbasids, this service also became an intelligence-gathering unit that kept track of those critical of the government. With access to such information, the caliphs could more easily thwart protests, rebellions, and other potential threats to the state. The head of the army also played a role on this front. Because there were few wars during the Abbasid period, his energies were often channeled into internal, police-like actions at home, and he became a widely feared figure in society.

Commerce and Trade

Baghdad became more than an extremely large city under Abbasid rule. It also became one of the most commercially busy and richest cities in the world. Its economy boomed primarily because Baghdad was a center of trade and a home to Muslim merchants who visited lands near and far, including India and China. In the words of noted historian W. H. McNeill, professor emeritus at the University of Chicago, "A powerful economic upsurge accompanied a relatively high level of peace and order. Merchants and artisans ministered to the refined tastes of the wealthy at home and developed trade with most of the lands of Eurasia [Asia and Europe combined]."

Among the thousands of products these traders brought to Baghdad were olive oil from Tunisia, rice and wheat from Egypt, iron from various parts of Europe, and tin from the faraway British Isles.

Muslim traders also daringly traveled south of the great Sahara Desert. There, in the vastness of north-central Africa, they found numerous, thriving kingdoms, both large and small. These merchants told the people they met about the relatively new faith of the Prophet from Mecca, and over time large numbers of Africans in this region and throughout the continent converted to Islam.

The expansion of trade also stimulated the rise of a banking industry among Muslims in Baghdad and other cities across the empire. The concept of buying items on credit spread far and wide. Even some of the caliphs borrowed from wealthy bankers in the capital, which the rulers paid back using taxes and other revenues derived from the imperial provinces.

Because so many long-range traders were traveling to Baghdad and around the empire, the Abbasid realm developed practical resources to enhance their activities. These included accurate maps; ocean-going sailing ships, like the *baghlah,* which could carry a large crew and plenty of cargo; and inns where merchants and other travelers, along with their pack animals, could rest and eat. The inns, called *caravanserai,* varied in size. The largest were so big that they could accommodate more than a thousand travelers and their animals. Such a facility also featured a mosque for worship, one or more shops, and a bathhouse, in addition to bedrooms, dining rooms, and stables.

Literary and Scientific Strides

The upsurge in long-distance travel and large-scale trade exposed the Arab world to other cultures and their ideas, an advancement that increased the sophistication of Islamic culture. One of the most important developments along these lines was a literary revolution. Through the influence of literate men who rose to prominence in the imperial bureaucracy, the rest of the upper class learned how to read and write. This breakthrough stimulated the production of literature, including stories, poetry, and historical accounts. The most famous of these works was the collection of myths entitled *The Book of One Thousand and One Nights,* which later became better known as *The Arabian Nights.*

Another advancement that grew out of increased exposure to the outside world—and enhanced literary culture—was the Arabs' adoption of Chinese paper-making practices. The Muslims took Chinese techniques and improved them, producing a relatively low-cost form of paper. This feat not only increased literary activity, but also catalyzed the establishment of book-making shops and libraries.

The most crucial factor driving the expansion of Islamic literature was the rediscovery and translation of ancient Greek literature.

An illustration from the *Maqāmāt* of al-Hariri. The *Maqāmāt,* completed during the thirteenth century and considered one of the greatest literary treasures of Arabic, is a collection of stories set around a roguish hero, Abu Zayd, who makes his living begging and swindling.

Under the caliph al-Mamun, who reigned from 813–833, hundreds of Greek (and Persian and Indian) works were translated into Arabic. Al-Mamun also founded the university-like Academy of Wisdom in Baghdad. According to Gaston Wiet, academic and late director of the Museum of Islamic Art in Cairo, "Scholars of all races and religions were invited to work there. They were concerned with preserving a universal heritage, which was not specifically Moslem and was Arabic only in language. [These intellectuals] eagerly set to work to discover the thoughts of antiquity [ancient times]."

The work accomplished at the Academy inspired numerous Muslim scholars. They soon began producing commentaries on the writings of Aristotle and other ancient philosophers and scientists.

Such commentaries rapidly gave way to more original Muslim achievements in a wide range of scientific disciplines. The mathematician al-Khwarizmi introduced so-called Arabic numerals (actually an improved version of Indian symbols) for use in calculation. A doctor named al-Razi wrote a large medical encyclopedia and performed experiments in the style of modern chemistry. The geographer al-Masudi penned a largely accurate description of the known world (then consisting of Asia, Africa, and Europe). And an astronomical observatory was erected in Baghdad. Among their long list of accomplishments, its operators made important improvements to the astrolabe invented by the ancient Greeks. (The astrolabe was a hand-held instrument that determined the positions of the heavenly bodies for telling time, surveying, and/or navigation.)

Abbasid scientists also made strides in zoology, cartography (map-making), and agriculture.

The Abbasid Golden Age was equally noteworthy for its achievements in the arts and architecture. Artisans in Baghdad and other cities across the empire turned out magnificent works of bronze and glass. They also created ceramics (pottery) of extremely high quality. Many of these ceramic items featured a special shiny glaze that inspired a number of Italian potters during the early years of Europe's famous Renaissance period. In addition, Muslim craftsmen produced beautiful illustrated literary manuscripts and miniature painted portraits.

Meanwhile, Islamic architecture, which had begun to develop in Umayyad times, reached new heights under the Abbasids. Muslim architects and builders borrowed certain architectural ideas from other cultures, notably the Byzantines, Persians, ancient Romans, and ancient Egyptians. However, they incorporated these foreign elements in a way that produced a unique and quite elegant form of new architecture.

An outstanding example of medieval Islamic architecture is the Great Mosque at Cordoba, in southern Spain, built during the late 700s. This sanctuary features a square-shaped interior with a hall containing hundreds of decorated columns. Above these pillars stretch a series of stylish curving arches. Later, another distinctive element of Islamic architecture was added to the Cordoba mosque: the minaret, a tower from which the muezzin calls people to prayer.

THE QUR'AN USED IN DECORATION

Another thematic element seen quite often in Islamic architecture is the decorative use of quotations from the Qur'an. Noted British professor of religion John Bowker describes this aspect in writing about a window in the Alhambra, an Islamic palace built in southern Spain:

> [The window] represents a splendid example of the ways in which Arabic script, particularly verses from the Quran, was used for decorative purposes. The actual window is surrounded by . . . Arabic script combined with abstract designs, forming a whole [that] creates the impression that the window is suspended from the arch above rather than supporting it. Above the colored tile [band] that frames the alcove [are] the words . . . "There is no conqueror other than God," repeated [many times].

The Patio de los Arrayanes at the Alhambra in Granada, Spain. An example of the country's most renowned Islamic art and architecture, the Alhambra was built by the Spanish Moors in the fourteenth century CE.

The End of an Age

The Islamic Golden Age eventually ended, along with the long-lived dynasty that had helped to generate it. The fall of the Abbasids in the mid-1200s came about for two main reasons. First, before that time there had been a general decline in Abbasid wealth and power. Over the course of several centuries large portions of the empire had seceded and formed independent Islamic states. These areas included Spain, parts of North Africa, and Anatolia (what is now Turkey), among others. This fragmentation significantly reduced the dynasty's influence and revenues.

Bigger, more sudden, and more destructive was the Mongol invasion in the 1240s and 1250s. An aggressive people from east-central Asia, the Mongols swept into and overran Iran, Iraq, and other Muslim lands. They sacked and burned the magnificent metropolis of Baghdad and killed most of its residents, as well as the last Abbasid ruler, al-Mustasim, and his family. What is more, the invaders destroyed the region's vast and elaborate irrigation system. This action ensured that the surviving inhabitants would not be able to recover for a long time.

Fortunately for Islam and its adherents, the faith did survive these and other setbacks that the Abbasid Empire and other

Arab nations suffered in the medieval era. (Among the most devastating was the loss of Spain to Christian armies in the 1400s.) Several successful Islamic empires, including that of the Ottomans in Turkey, rose from the ashes of the Mongol incursions. And in the twentieth century a number of modern Muslim nations emerged. Their populations still celebrate pivotal moments from the period lasting from Muhammad's revelations to the Golden Age. Muslims everywhere look back proudly on those fateful years in which the faith was born and its early followers shaped the course of human history.

The Abbasid Palace in Baghdad, Iraq

Timeline

	BCE	
	224	Ardishir I deposes the last king of Parthia, in Iran, and establishes the Sassanian Empire.

	CE	
	476	The western portion of the Roman Empire collapses; the eastern sector, centered at Constantinople, survives and steadily mutates into the Byzantine Empire.
	ca. 500	The town of Mecca, in western Arabia, has become a major religious center.
	527-565	Reign of the Byzantine emperor Justinian, who recaptures some of the lost western Roman lands.
	570	Muhammad is born in Mecca.
	610	Muhammad receives his first divine revelation in a cave near Mecca.

612	The Sassanian king Khusrau II captures Jerusalem, then controlled by the Byzantines.
619	Muhammad's wife, Khadija, dies.
622	Muhammad flees from Mecca to Medina, an event that becomes known as the *Hijra*.
623	Muhammad marries Aisha, daughter of Abu Bakr.
624	Muhammad changes the direction faced during Muslim prayer from Jerusalem to Mecca; his followers attack Mecca.
627	The Meccans assault Medina in retaliation; the Byzantines attack the Sassanian capital of Ctesiphon.
629	Muhammad and his followers take charge of Mecca.
632	Muhammad dies at age sixty-three; Abu Bakr becomes caliph.
634	Bakr dies; Umar becomes caliph.
636	The Arabs defeat the Byzantines at Yarmouk, in Syria.

644	Umar is assassinated; Uthman becomes caliph.
656	Uthman is murdered; Ali becomes the fourth caliph; Ali defeats a group of rebels in the Battle of the Camel.
658	Ali defeats the Kharijites.
661	Ali is assassinated; Muawiya becomes the first Umayyad caliph.
661-750	Years of the Umayyad dynasty of caliphs.
666	Libya falls to Muslim armies.
680	Muawiya dies; his son, Yazid, becomes caliph; Yazid's soldiers kill Hussein, grandson of Muhammad.
711	Muslim forces begin to enter Spain.
717-720	Reign of Umar II, who attempts to introduce controversial domestic reforms.

718	The Muslims invade what is now southern France.
732	Frankish chieftain Charles Martel defeats the Muslims near Poitiers.
750	The Umayyad dynasty falls and is replaced by the Abbasid dynasty.
763	The capital of the Abbasid realm moves from Syria to Baghdad, in Iraq.
813-833	Reign of the Abbasid caliph al-Mamun, who orders ancient Greek literary works to be translated into Arabic.
1258	The Mongols sack and burn Baghdad, ending the Abbasid dynasty.

Sources

Chapter One: The Middle East Before Islam

p. 13:   "worship one God . . ." Tamara Sonn, *A Brief History of Islam* (Malden, MA: Blackwell, 2010), xix.

p. 15:   "We order all bishops . . ." Justinian, *Novella,* quoted in Medieval Sourcebook, "Regulating Church Ritual," http://www.fordham.edu/halsall/source/justinian-nov137.html.

p. 18:   "Do ye, Ahura . . ." A. T. Olmstead, *History of the Persian Empire* (Chicago: University of Chicago Press, 1974), 97.

p. 20:   "Mecca had already . . ." Richard Hooker, "Pre-Islamic Arab Culture," http://wsu.edu/~dee/ISLAM/PRE.HTM.

p. 21:   "The Jews and Christians . . ." Karen Armstrong, *Islam: A Short History* (New York: Modern Library, 2000), 3.

Chapter Two: Emergence of the Final Prophet

p. 23:   "poised to step out . . ." Lesley Hazleton, *After the Prophet: The Epic Story of the Shia-Sunni Split in Islam* (New York: Doubleday, 2009), 7.

p. 24:   "skillfully melded faith and finance . . ." Ibid., 14.

p. 26:   "I was standing . . ." Efraim Karsh, *Islamic Imperialism: A History* (New Haven: Yale University Press, 2006), 9.

p. 26:   "What shall I recite? . . ." Ibid.

p. 26:   "Recite in the name . . ." Qur'an 96.1–5.

p. 27:   "Surely We revealed it . . ." Qur'an 97.1–5.

p. 30:   "Certain aspects of Muhammad's preaching . . ." Karsh, *Islamic Imperialism,* 10–11.

p. 31:   "a watershed in Islamic history . . ." Ibid., 111–12.

Chapter Three: Basic Beliefs and Rituals

p. 37: "They [Muslims] are one community . . ." A. Guillaume, *The Life of Muhammad—A Translation of Ishaq's Sirat Rasul Allah* (Karachi: Oxford University Press, 1955), 231–233, quoted in The Constitutional Society, "The Medina Charter," http://www.constitution.org/cons/medina/con_medina.htm.

p. 38: "Muhammad protected the settlement . . ." Armstrong, *Islam,* 20.

pp. 39-40: "The community had suddenly lost . . ." Paul Lunde, *Islam: Faith, Culture, History* (New York: Dorling Kindersley, 2002), 23.

pp. 40-41: "Allah is He besides Whom . . ." Qur'an 2.255.

p. 42: "[They will wear] garments of fire . . ." Qur'an 22.19–22.

p. 42: "Surely Allah will make . . ." Qur'an 22.23.

p. 43: "I testify that there is . . ." *Encyclopedia Britannica Online, s.v. "shahadah,"* http://www.britannica.com/EBchecked/topic/537735/shahadah.

p. 44: "God is the most Great . . ." Lunde, *Islam,* 19.

p. 45: "Now, as in the past . . ." Neal Robinson, *Islam: A Concise Introduction* (Washington, DC: Georgetown University Press, 1999), 148.

Chapter Four: The Early Caliphs and Expansion

p. 48:   "In everything that was to follow . . ." Hazleton, *After the Prophet,* 13.

p. 48:   "The time approaches . . ." Ibid., 51.

p. 50:   "This vision . . ." Karsh, *Islamic Imperialism,* 22–23.

p. 50:   "When people possess . . ." Ibid., 23.

pp. 52-53: "[The Byzantine emperor] Heraclius gathered . . ." Medieval Sourcebook, "The Battle of Yarmouk," http://www.fordham.edu/halsall/source/yarmuk.html.

p. 53:   "Allah has made . . ." Karsh, *Islamic Imperialism,* 24.

p. 53:   "Without [Umar's approach] . . ." Patricia Crone, "The Rise of Islam in the World," in *The Cambridge Illustrated History of the Islamic World*, ed. Francis Robinson (New York: Cambridge University Press, 1996), 11–12.

p. 54:   "There was nothing religious . . ." Armstrong, *Islam,* 29–30.

Chapter Five: Divisions Among the Faithful

p. 57:   "I am the City . . ." Hazleton, *After the Prophet,* 35.

p. 61:   "The accounts are confused . . ." Ibid., 112.

pp. 63-64: "You must create in your mind . . ." *Nahj ul Balagha,* "Letter 53," http://www.nahjulbalagha.org/LetterDetail.php?Letter=53.

p. 64:   "O my Allah . . ." *Nahj ul Balagha,* "Sermon 170," http://www.nahjulbalagha.org/SermonDetail.php?Sermon=170

p. 65:   "they refused to accept the arbitration . . ." Armstrong, *Islam,* 35.

Chapter Six: Rise and Fall of the Umayyads

p. 71: "After a short battle . . ." Karsh, *Islamic Imperialism,* 36.

p. 71: "The killing of the Prophet's grandson . . ." Erica Fraser, "The Battle of Karbala," http://www.ucalgary.ca/applied_history/tutor/islam/caliphate/

pp. 72-73: "Islam was [very] closely connected . . ." Richard Hooker, "Civil War and the Umayyads," http://wsu.edu/~dee/ISLAM/UMAY.HTM.

p. 74: "The Arabs [were successful] . . ." Christon I. Archer et al., *World History of Warfare* (Lincoln: University of Nebraska Press, 2008), 128.

p. 76: "The Moslem horsemen dashed . . ." Leon Bernard and Theodore B. Hodges, eds., *Readings in European History* (New York: Macmillan, 1961), 85.

pp. 77-78: "these reforms came too late . . ." Lunde, *Islam,* 53.

Chapter Seven: The Abbasids and Golden Age

pp. 81-82: "one of the most momentous . . ." Karsh, *Islamic Imperialism,* 44.

pp. 82-83: "The core of the city . . ." Lunde, *Islam,* 54.

p. 83: "The city of Baghdad formed . . ." Medieval Sourcebook, "Yakut: Baghdad Under the Abbasids," http://www.fordham.edu/halsall/source/1000baghdad.html.

p. 86: "A powerful economic upsurge . . ." W. H. McNeill, *The Rise of the West: A History of the Human Community* (Chicago: University of Chicago Press, 1992), 474–475.

p. 89: "Scholars of all races . . ." Gaston Wiet, "The Golden Age of Arab and Islamic Culture," http://www.khamush.com/sufism/golden.htm.

p. 91: "[The window] represents . . ." John Bowker, *World Religions: The Great Faiths Explored and Explained* (London: Dorling Kindersley, 1997), 167.

Bibliography

Selected Books

Armstrong, Karen. *Islam: A Short History.* New York: Modern Library, 2000.

Aslan, Reza. *No God but God: The Origins, Evolution, and Future of Islam.* New York: Random House, 2005.

Belt, Don, ed. *The World of Islam.* Washington, DC: National Geographic, 2001.

Crone, Patricia. *Meccan Trade and the Rise of Islam.* Oxford: Blackwell, 1987.

Gordon, Matthew S. *Islam: Origins, Practices, Holy Texts, Sacred Persons, Sacred Places.* New York: Oxford University Press, 2002.

Hazleton, Lesley. *After the Prophet: The Epic Story of the Shia-Sunni Split in Islam.* New York: Doubleday, 2009.

Hodgson, Marshall G. S. *The Venture of Islam: Volume 1, The Classical Age of Islam.* Chicago: University of Chicago Press, 1977.

Ibn Ishaq, Muhammad. *The Life of Muhammad.* Oxford: Oxford University Press, 1955.

Karsh, Efraim. *Islamic Imperialism: A History.* New Haven: Yale University Press, 2006.

Kennedy, Hugh. *The Great Arab Conquests: How the Spread of Islam Changed the World We Live In.* Cambridge, MA: Da Capo, 2008.

Lewis, Bernard. *The Arabs in History.* New York: Oxford University Press, 2002.

————. *Islam in History.* Chicago: Open Court, 2001.

Lunde, Paul. *Islam: Faith, Culture, History.* New York: Dorling Kindersley, 2002.

Nasr, Seyyed, H. *Islam: Religion, History, and Civilization.* New York: HarperOne, 2002.

Payne, Robert. *The History of Islam.* New York: Dorset Press, 1995.

Robinson, Francis, ed. *The Cambridge Illustrated History of the Islamic World.* New York: Cambridge University Press, 1996.

Robinson, Neal. *Islam: A Concise Introduction.* Washington, DC: Georgetown University Press, 1999.

Sonn, Tamara. *A Brief History of Islam.* Malden, MA: Blackwell, 2010.

Glossary

adhan: The Islamic call to prayer.

ahl al-kitab: "The people of the book"; Muslims, Jews, and Christians, all of whom recognize holy scriptures.

Allah: The Arabic word for God.

ayat: A verse of the Qur'an.

baghlah: An ocean-going ship often used by Muslim traders.

Bedouins (or Bedu): Arabs who lived a nomadic lifestyle.

caliph: In medieval times, the ruler of the Muslim community or empire.

caliphate: The office of the caliph; in upper case (Caliphate), it refers to the medieval Islamic empire.

caravanserai: Inns for traders and other travelers.

din: A monotheistic faith.

dynasty: A family line of rulers.

Five Pillars of Islam: Major rituals performed by all devout Muslims.

Hajj: One of Islam's Five Pillars: A pilgrimage to Mecca performed at least once in a person's lifetime.

hanif: In medieval Mecca, men who went on solitary retreats into the wilderness.

Hijra (or Hegira): Muhammad's flight from Mecca to Medina in A.D. 622.

Jazirat al-Arab: "Island of the Arabs"; the ancient Arab name for the Arabian Peninsula.

jihad: "Struggle"; a personal or social struggle; or a holy war.

Kaaba: Located in Mecca, the large cube viewed by Muslims as Islam's holiest site.

Kharijites: A sect of Islam whose members are very conservative and purist.

kuttab: Administrative and other assistants to the *wazir*.

Laylat al-Qadr: "Night of Power"; the night during which Muhammad received his first revelation.

Maghrib: "The west"; more specifically a medieval Muslim reference to the region of coastal North Africa.

malak: An angel.

mawali: In medieval times, non-Arab converts to Islam.

minaret: A tower, often adjoining a mosque, from which the muezzin calls the faithful to prayer.

muezzin: A mosque official who performs the *adhan*.

qibla: The direction a Muslim faces while praying.

Qur'an (or Koran): The sacred book of Islam, said to have been dictated to Muhammad by the angel Gabriel.

salah (or salat): One of Islam's Five Pillars: The recital of ritual prayers five times each day.

sawm: One of Islam's Five Pillars: Fasting during the holy month of Ramadan.

shahadah: One of Islam's Five Pillars: A statement of belief.

Shia (or Shiites): A major sect of Islam; they believe that Ali, the fourth caliph, was the first legitimate ruler to follow Muhammad.

Sunni: A major sect of Islam; they hold that the first three caliphs who followed Muhammad were legitimate.

sura: A chapter of the Qur'an.

ummah (or umma): The Muslim community.

wazir (or vizier): The chief administrator in the government of many medieval Islamic states.

zakat: One of Islam's Five Pillars: Giving charity to the poor.

Zoroastrianism: The religion followed by members of the upper classes and others in ancient Persia.

Web Sites

The Arabian Nights
http://www.sacred-texts.com/neu/burt1k1/

Islamic History
http://www.fordham.edu/halsall/islam/islamsbook.html

The Holy Qur'an. Translated by M. H. Shakir. University of Michigan Library.
http://quod.lib.umich.edu/k/koran/

The Life of Muhammad
http://www.pbs.org/muhammad/timeline_html.shtml

Mecca
http://www.sacredsites.com/middle_east/saudi_arabia/mecca.html

Medieval Muslim Travelers and Mapmakers
http://www.sfusd.k12.ca.us/schwww/sch618/Travelers/Islamic_
        Travelers_and_Mapm.html

Index

Photo Credits

2: Courtesy of Ilmarry

7: Courtesy of Wotan

8-9: Russell Kord / Alamy

10: Courtesy of Enzuru

12: Used under license from iStockphoto.com

16-17: North Wind Picture Archives / Alamy

25: Courtesy of Nazli

28-29: Courtesy of Crystalina

32-33: Courtesy of Mystic

34: Courtesy of NormanEinstein

40-41: Used under license from iStockphoto.com

44: Courtesy of Muhammad Mahdi Karim

46: Russell Kord / Alamy

50-51: Used under license from iStockphoto.com

52: Courtesy of Mohammad adil

56: Used under license from iStockphoto.com

59: Courtesy of Ahmad Reza Haraji

62-63: Used under license from iStockphoto.com

67: Courtesy of the U.S. Navy

68-69: EmmePi Travel / Alamy

73: Courtesy of Gabagool

78-79: Courtesy of Jerzy Strzelecki

80-81: nik wheeler / Alamy

88: Lebrecht Music and Arts Photo Library / Alamy

91 Bottom: Courtesy of Jan Zeschky

92: Courtesy of Murraytheb

93: Courtesy of Jim Gordon

Book cover and interior design by Derrick Carroll Creative.